KU-754-368

What do you like to wear?

Do your clothes hang loose?

Get Dressed!

Gwenyth Swain

small world

To find out more about the pictures in this book, turn to page 22.
To find out more about sharing this book with children, turn to page 24.

The photographs in this book are reproduced through the courtesy of: © CORBIS Royalty Free, front cover and p. 4; © Glacial Lakes and Prairies of Northeastern South Dakota, back cover and p. 7; © Tiziana and Gianni Baldizzone/CORBIS, p. 1; © Todd Gipstein/CORBIS, P. 3; © Dean Conger/CORBIS, pp. 5, 15; © CORBIS Royalty Free, p. 6; © Julie Habel/CORBIS, p. 8; © David and Peter Tumley/CORBIS, p. 9; © Jodi Jacobson/Peter Arnold, p. 10; © Morton Beebe, S.F./CORBIS, p. 11; © Penny Tweedie/CORBIS, p. 12; © Françoise Gervais/CORBIS, p. 13; © Pablo Corral V/CORBIS, p. 14; © Reflections Photolibrary/ CORBIS, pp. 16, 18; © Laura Dwight/CORBIS, p. 17; © Phil Schermeister/CORBIS, p. 19; © Philip Gould/CORBIS, p. 20; © Liba Taylor/CORBIS, p. 21.

Copyright © 2002 by Gwenyth Swain

All rights reserved.

No part of the publication may be reproduced or utilized in any form or by any means, electronic or mechanical, including photocopying, recording or by any information retrieval system, without the prior written permission of the publishers.

First published in Great Britain in 2002 by
Zero to Ten Limited, 327 High Street, Slough, Sl1 1TX
By arrangement with First Avenue Editions

First published in the United States in 2002 by
First Avenue Editions, an imprint of Lerner Publishing Group
241 First Avenue North, Minneapolis, MN 55401 U.S.A.

A CIP catalogue record for this book is available from the British Library.

ISBN: 1-84089-232-3

Manufactured in the United States of America
1 2 3 4 5 6 – JR – 07 06 05 04 03 02

DUDLEY PUBLIC LIBRARIES
L 46138
636120   SCH
J 391

Do they hug you tight?

Does a special outfit make
you look just right?

Pick clothes to fit you
and the things you do.

Pull on a parka to play in the snow.

Cover yourself, but
let your smile show.

Choose clothes with care
when you want to stay cool.

Slip into a swimsuit and splash at the pool.

Beads and paint say it's your big day.

The slant of a hat says it's time to play.

Grab clean, dry clothes
fresh from the line.

Pull them on or iron them.
You'll look fine.

Tug on your zip. Cover your toes.

Loop and pull to make a neat bow.

Button that button.

Fasten that dickey bow.

Get ready. Get dressed!

Add a smile. Look your best.

More about the Pictures

Front cover and page 4: Loose clothing keeps friends cool in the hot climate of Tanzania, in East Africa.

Back cover and page 7: A young Native American powwow dancer performs in South Dakota, USA.

Page 1: A Rabari girl is dressed for her naming ceremony in the state of Gujarat in western India.

Page 3: A girl in Beijing, China, wears her school uniform – and a smile.

Page 5: A toddler is bundled up tight for a winter day in Irkutsk, Russia.

Page 6: Two girls on the Indonesian island of Bali wear ceremonial dresses and headdresses.

Page 8: Children in Iowa, USA, dress warmly to play in the snow.

Page 9: A young girl in Tehran, Iran, wears *hijab,* or Islamic clothing, that covers all but her face and hands. The word *hijab* comes from the Arabic word for modesty.

Page 10: A girl in New Jersey, USA, picks an outfit for a hot summer's day.

Page 11: A young girl floats on a raft in a swimming pool in Puerto Vallarta, Mexico.

Page 12: These two Aboriginal boys in Arnhem Land, a region in northern Australia, are dressed for a ceremony.

Page 13: Girls play dress up in Maine, USA.

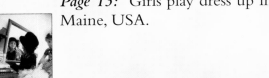

Page 14: Clothes dry on the line outside a traditional house along the Tomebamba River in Cuenca, Ecuador.

Page 15: A West Indian girl carries a bundle of laundry on her head in Grenadines, in the Caribbean.

Page 16: This young girl is just learning to pull socks snug over her toes.

Page 17: This African American boy knows how to tie his shoelaces. Do you know how?

Page 18: A girl in Britain buttons her school blazer.

Page 19: Boys on North Caicos Island in the Bahamas help each other look their best for their school-leaving ceremony.

Page 20: In Saint George, Bermuda, two eight-year-olds start the day right in neat, clean clothes.

Page 21: In the Gambia, in West Africa, a girl keeps her head covered and her smile bright.

A Note to Adults on Sharing This Book

Help your child become a lifelong reader. Read this book together, taking turns as you both read out loud. Look over the photographs and choose your favourites. Sound out new words and come back to them later to look at them again. Then try these 'extensions' – activities that extend the experience of reading and build discussion and problem-solving skills.

Talk about Getting Dressed

All around the world, people wear clothes that suit the weather and suit the things they do. Ask your child to describe the clothing people wear in this book. How do the outfits differ from what your child wears? How are they the same? Ask your child why children in different parts of the world wear different clothes. What kinds of outfits shown in the book would your child like to wear for a change?

Make a Paper 'Wardrobe'

With your child, gather pictures of people dressed in different ways. Copy photographs of yourself as a child wearing your favourite outfits. Ask your child to cut out pictures of unusual-looking clothes from magazines. Then put all the pictures together in a scrapbook. Think of this book as a paper "wardrobe." Ask your child what clothes he or she would take out of the wardrobe and wear in the summer or winter, at Halloween or to school, or for a party or special event.

DUDLEY SCHOOLS
LIBRARY SERVICE

Schools Library and Information Services
S00000636120